I Remember Fairbanks and Skibo

I Remember
Fairbanks and Skibo

John A. Lauerer

Eastern Itascan Company
Nashwauk, Minnesota

Edited by Steven D. Harsin

Photographs from John A. Lauerer collection reproduced by
Iron Range Research Center,
Chisholm, Minnesota

Book Design by Joyce Peraaho

Copyright © 1994 John A. Lauerer

First Edition

Published by arrangement with John A. Lauerer

Distributed by John A. Lauerer

Library of Congress Catalog Card No. 94-061703

ISBN: 0-9636894-1-X

Published in the United States of America by
Eastern Itascan Company
310 Central Avenue
Nashwauk, Minnesota 55769-1132

Printed in the United States of America

Contents

Wilma and John Lauerer on their wedding day, June 30, 1939

To My Family

My dear wife, Wilma, is painfully absent from this memoir of my youth, yet she has been a critical element in my success. Without her trust and encouragement, my story may have been very different. Our partnership has spanned 55 wonderful years.

This book is dedicated to my wife, Wilma, my daughters, Kathy and Joan, and my grandchildren, Paul, Leah, John and Erin.

John Lauerer, 1932

Prologue

The world has changed so much since I was a young boy. Today, our news is dominated by "bang bang gangs," drug problems and violence. In the days of my youth, such problems were unknown, at least to a young boy.

When my family emigrated to the United States of America, we were embarking on an adventure into the unknown. My parents were brave souls to bring their little sons into a remote wilderness halfway around the globe. I don't think people today can understand what those immigrants went through to find a better life for themselves and their children. Today, everything comes so easily, we have no means to comprehend the challenges those people faced.

It is my hope in writing this book, that I can expose the reader to a little of what life was like in a Minnesota white-pine logging community during the early part of this century. We were immigrants, carving ourselves a niche in the strange, wild forests of North America. Today, those forests are gone, as is the lifestyle we led. Because there are few left today who can remember Fairbanks as I do, I feel it is my duty to record what I remember, even though I don't feel I can do justice to those wonderful people who exerted such a powerful influence on my early development.

John Lauerer

CHAPTER 1

Coming to a New Home

I was born in Bavaria, Germany, in the first decade of the Twentieth Century. When one year old, I walked with my brother, Joe, up the gang plank of the Zealand liner in Liverpool, England. We were setting sail for the new world properly attired in new, matching sailor suits. My parents were brave enough to take their sons on an adventure just 30 days after the world's worst passenger ship accident, the sinking of the Titanic.

June, 1912 broke all records for the number of icebergs in the North Atlantic, the most dangerous and numerous floe of icebergs off Newfoundland for all time. Within a day or two of land, our ship passed over the 1,517 bodies two miles down on the ocean floor. The masters of the Zealand wound through the icebergs more slowly than the Titanic, proceeding with caution because they knew what had happened recently and were trying to cross safely and not trying to break all-time records for crossing.

Our ship, too, hit an iceberg. The water pumps were switched on and went to work sending the water in the boat back out to sea. The lifeboats on our ship were kept safe and dry on board with plenty of room for all 2,000 souls on board. Our ship made it safely to Ellis Island, so the name John Lauerer can still be seen on the roster of immigrants that came to the land of freedom in 1912.

Fairbanks, Minnesota, is where I settled with my family as a one-year-old immigrant. This town, about 18 miles south of Aurora, was both a mill town and a logging town in the midst of the white pine still left as virgin in the Superior National Forest. Fairbanks was just a bit too much like one of those wild-west towns we enjoy so much in the movies. The not-too-gentle people, the strict family life, the good and bad teachers, the too-strict Catholic upbringing, the mill hands and the lumber jacks shaped me into the personality and man I became.

Lauerer family (left to right): Theresa (mother), Katherine, Joe, John (on ground), Joseph (father). Joe and John are wearing the matching sailor suits they wore on the voyage to America.

The log cabin we moved into left much to be desired. The main cabin had three rooms. One big room served as the combination living room, dining room and kitchen. There were two bedrooms but no door for either of them. There was a second cabin built perpendicular against the first. This one was used as a kitchen during the summer months. The inside of the cabin did not have the bare logs exposed. The walls and ceiling were finished with good but unpainted lumber. My dad painted the inside of the entire cabin pink. After he got the whole thing painted, he discovered that he had used two different shades of pink. He had to repaint some of it with a second coat to make it match.

In our cabin, things were humble, as one would expect. Our home, of course, had no electricity, phone or appliances. There was one table in the middle of the room. There was one oil lamp with a flat wick placed in the oil and the opposite end lighted. This lamp was very important and was kept burning at low ebb all night. There were no lamps in the bedrooms. The rays of light from the one lamp in the big room was all the bedrooms had. I recall one occasion the lamp went out. The total darkness was a shock, and I can remember crying about it.

I enrolled in a one-room school before I was five years old with only a knowledge of German and very few words of English, yet I skipped the sixth grade because my teacher then did not want to have to teach a grade with only one pupil. My first teacher had greater success with me than all the rest of the teachers I had from that first year forward through the three colleges I attended.

When I left the one-room school with a total enrollment of 18 in the rough, wild, pioneer town of Fairbanks to go to high school, I had to succeed at making the supreme adjustment in my life to date. I had to leave my parents and home for the first time in my life.

I enrolled in a class in Aurora with 50 other students. Going to a different room every hour and having five different teachers seemed such a problem and my world became so confusing. I must have met all the requirements for a school dropout. I resisted the impulse to flee, partly because to get home I would have to ride on two different trains. I put up one of the great fights of my life. Finally, the first day ended. On the second and third days, I became aware of how friendly these new "strangers" were getting to be. It seemed that I was being accepted 100 percent. This gave me great strength and helped me relate with confidence to the adults in the town. In less than two years, I was elected by the class members to be the toast-master for the greatest event in the city, the Junior-Senior Banquet.

Although I was not permitted to go out for football in Aurora because of the risk of injury, I made good progress in high school. I went out for oratory, took big parts in plays and joined the glee club. I graduated in the upper half of my class and was the youngest student that ever graduated from Aurora up to that year.

When I enrolled in Eveleth Junior College, I went out for football and made the squad within the first two weeks. I remember starting at least one game and playing 60 minutes therein. In those years, there was no platoon system, meaning I played every minute on offense and defense.

In the early 1980s, I joined the Iron Range Historical Society. That Society wanted a history of the Cadotte Lake sawmill in Fairbanks. A man was referred to me as the only man alive who had a first-hand, clear memory of all the details of my personal life, and he was very pleased with my work. The man had my age, but not my health. He died suddenly before the project was completed. Fortunately, I made copies of much of the work I did for him.

I still experience a special thrill when I write to people in such cities as Eveleth and Aurora. I also experience pleasure when I so frequently find myself in the company of almost anybody from the great Iron Range area.

CHAPTER 2

Life in Fairbanks

I consider the mouth of the St. Louis River near Cloquet to be the gateway to the Arrowhead and Iron Range areas of northeastern Minnesota. The voyagers and fur traders were familiar with Lake Superior and were the first white men to discover this route. Most of the credit for opening the area around the Iron Range goes to Jean Baptiste Cadotte, a Frenchman. The lake in Fairbanks that fed the logs into the sawmill there is called Lake Cadotte. Cadotte was active in the fur trading industry. He married the most admired Indian maiden and produced three little Cadottes, who later attended college in eastern Canada. When the English threatened to remove the French head of the fort, the Chippewa threatened to go to war. Jean Baptiste Cadotte stayed. This great Frenchman has his name emblazoned on a huge plaque on the banks of the St. Louis River in Cloquet at Spaford Park, a historic island that is one of my favorite stopping places for picnics. According to some, this island had many saloons and no women, except prostitutes, ever went on this island.

In 1854-1855, the Tri-band Chippewa liquidation of title of land in northeastern Minnesota occurred. This treaty was broken like nearly all the others the white man signed with the original Americans. This treaty, however, was reincarnated only after the white man ruined much of the land through deforestation and killed most of the largest collection of fur-bearing animals in the world, two of the most precious being now almost extinct — the martin and fisher.

In 1865, there was a gold rush to Lake Vermilion. A canoe route had already been established up the St. Louis River with a portage to the Pike River and then to Lake Vermilion. This was the route no doubt used to get to the only two fur trading posts actually inside the borders of Minnesota. There were many other trading posts, but they were on the border, usually on rivers or lakes.

The year 1884 was very important not only to my life, but also to my family's life. Twenty-six years before my birth, the railroad was completed through Fairbanks from Tower to Two Harbors and Duluth. The same year, the first shipment of ore was hauled from Ely through Skibo (*pronounced Skĭ´bō*) and Fairbanks on to the ship loading docks at Two Harbors. In those days, if someone wanted to travel or transport things faster than horses could walk, the railroad steam engine was the only alternate mode of movement.

That dear Duluth and Iron Range Railway (D&IRR) not only gave birth to the Cadotte Fairbanks sawmill, but three decades later "gave" me money for five summers in order to complete my high school education and to get far into college. If it were not for the mill and the railroad, Fairbanks would, of course, never have grown into a vibrant, typical, western frontier community of some 300 people. For at least a quarter-century, the mill and the extra-large, white-pine logging camp two-thirds mile west of Fairbanks were magnets, drawing evermore people to come thither and pulsate additional life and pep into those who first came upon the scene.

The large, three-stack steam mill, the attached planer mill and the most extensive facilities for drying, curing and storing lumber I have ever seen, in life or pictures, made up much of Fairbanks. The mill was built by J.A. Robb and Frank S. Colvin, two of the best and greatest lumbermen on the Iron Range. They operated the mill until 1905, when it was purchased by Doctor Lenont from Virginia, Minn., and who ran the mill until about 1921.

The railroad divided Fairbanks into two areas. All the mill facilities and most of the homes for the mill people were east of the railroad and on the opposite side of the downtown section. All of the town on the east side of the tracks, except the section house, was blessed with electricity furnished by a huge dynamo in the engine room of the sawmill. The hotel, the school and the Lauerer cabin, among others, were all on the opposite side of the tracks.

Looking north past the Duluth & Iron Range Railway switchyard at Fairbanks.

The electric power plant was in the engine room of the sawmill. This dynamo was fueled mostly by bark and lumber trash. It produced electricity for all the buildings that were related to the sawmill and the sawmill itself, the huge and well-light lumber yard, the large horse barn, and the homes of the people who lived off the production of the sawmill and the planer mill. I always marveled when going through that engine room, so big that it needed those three large smokestacks. I have never since seen three stacks on a mill, not even in pictures. I believe the third stack was for the large dynamo.

The section house was the only building east of the tracks that had no electricity. None of the buildings west of the tracks had electricity, including the log cabin in which I was raised. The important buildings, such as the depot, the station warehouse, the bar-hotel, the general store, and the school, all had either kerosene, carbide or gas lights; none had electric. In those that had electricity, the wiring was all done simply, using no conduit or armored cable. The wiring was not hidden inside the walls, the wires were just run along the ceiling. I do not recall seeing any appliances, and I believe electric power was used only for lighting.

Rows of lumber piled for drying and awaiting shipment beside the railroad spurs. In the background, note the very long building which contained the depot waiting room, the telegraph and train control office, and the long warehouse for storage of received and outgoing cargo. In front of the depot is the tallest pole in town. This pole had a steel ladder for servicing the kerosene lamp with red and green reflectors, which were used as indicators to stop trains or allow them to go through. The two-story building right of center is the hotel, bar, dining room, pool room, sitting and waiting room. The hotel was moved to this site in 1919. Next to the hotel is the ice house and to the right of it is the town pump. The low building to the right of center of the photograph is the Lauerer's log cabin. Further right is the home of the "pump man" who filled the water tanks on the steam engines. Trains always stopped for water, but never needed additional coal. The water came from a man-made ditch that ran from Lake Cadotte to several big tanks.

There was an office building for the mill and related functions, residences for mill personnel, a large two-story boarding house mostly for singles, a recreation building that had room for a pool table, and a large barn for 12 horses.

Most of the buildings were never painted. They developed the color that buildings get, kind of a dirty gray, from the sun and the rain.

Of all the buildings involved with the sawmill and the workers who worked there, none remain standing except two

8

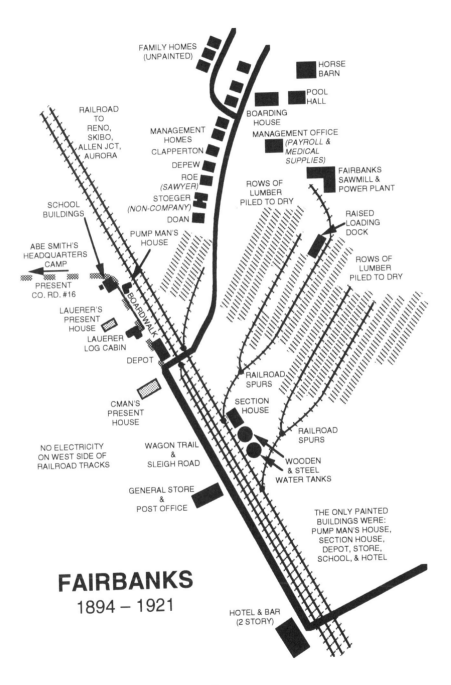

FAMILY HOMES
(UNPAINTED)

HORSE
BARN

POOL
HALL

RAILROAD
TO
RENO,
SKIBO,
ALLEN JCT,
AURORA

BOARDING
HOUSE

MANAGEMENT
HOMES
CLAPPERTON

MANAGEMENT OFFICE
(PAYROLL &
MEDICAL
SUPPLIES)

DEPEW

ROE
(SAWYER)

ROWS OF
LUMBER
PILED TO DRY

FAIRBANKS
SAWMILL &
POWER PLANT

SCHOOL
BUILDINGS

STOEGER
(NON-COMPANY)

DOAN

RAISED
LOADING
DOCK

ABE SMITH'S
HEADQUARTERS
CAMP

PUMP MAN'S
HOUSE

ROWS OF
LUMBER
PILED TO DRY

PRESENT
CO. RD. #16

LAUERER'S
PRESENT
HOUSE

LAUERER
LOG CABIN

DEPOT

RAILROAD
SPURS

CMAN'S
PRESENT
HOUSE

SECTION
HOUSE

NO ELECTRICITY
ON WEST SIDE OF
RAILROAD TRACKS

WAGON TRAIL
&
SLEIGH ROAD

RAILROAD
SPURS

WOODEN
& STEEL
WATER TANKS

GENERAL STORE
&
POST OFFICE

THE ONLY PAINTED
BUILDINGS WERE:
PUMP MAN'S HOUSE,
SECTION HOUSE,
DEPOT, STORE,
SCHOOL, & HOTEL

FAIRBANKS
1894 – 1921

HOTEL & BAR
(2 STORY)

9

homes. One has been rebuilt and moved across town. The second one is the home in which I lived after our first log cabin home was torn down to make room for Highway 16. This second Lauerer home was not changed except that it was moved down from the hill, across the railroad tracks and painted before our family moved out of the log cabin and into the new home. It is still the same as when I lived in it.

The general store, owned by Katherine and Sebastian Huber (center), was the second two-story business in Fairbanks. Katherine Huber was Theresa Lauerer's sister, and the Hubers sponsored the Joseph Lauerer family when they immigrated to America in 1912. Without their help, the struggle to survive in this white pine wilderness of America could have been ever so much more difficult.

George Loren Huber and his sister Katherine Huber outside the Fairbanks Hotel and Bar

The bar and school were as far apart as possible. It was the law that liquor could not be sold within a quarter-mile of the school, so the children would not be harmed by drunks. The hotel actually ended up out of town and in a dismal, very soft swamp. There was a long, clay, wagon road that was also the walking trail from town to the hotel and bar. The very impressive, two-story hotel had a pool room, a bar, and a large, elegant dining room. This building had, of course, a good hot water heating system with radiators and such.

When the Eighteenth Amendment forbade the sale of liquor in 1919, moving day for the big hotel building loomed. Since the law which formerly prevented the hotel's being in town no longer applied, the building could be brought across the soft swamp. I really enjoyed watching the moving of such a building. It had to be done when there was three feet of frost in the swamp. The means of power for moving the building was a windlass or turnstile apparatus with wire cable and a horse walking around the drum on which the cable wound. This horse pulled a pole fastened to the drum. This made the

George Loren Huber on the steps of the Fairbanks Hotel and Bar

cable pull the building. At one point, the building had to be pulled uphill to the great concern of those involved.

There was still work to be done once the building arrived in town. The hotel had been painted a beautiful shade of red, but had to be repainted. Apparently, after heavy drinking, some men did not bother to use the toilet, if there even were any in the rooms. At least there was much evidence that many men used the window, with the result that the building had to be painted to cover the streaks of urine coming down from the window sills.

Sometimes it seems wasteful that our modern motels and

hotels have chambermaids change the sheets every night, even though one sleeps in the same bed. I know the changing of bed sheets every night was not part of our culture, or at least was not practiced at every hotel in the Arrowhead Region in 1919. I recall a time when we witnessed this first hand. My dad took me, my brother and a friend named Gordon Erickson to Duluth. Two businessmen who had a business on Lake Avenue recommended a good hotel located between Fifth Avenue West and Lake Avenue on Superior Street. In the morning, one of us boys picked up a handful of toenails from the bed sheets. I can still recall this hotel clearly, even the name plate over the sidewalk which read, "Eldorado."

I know I am not the only man who ever considered his mother to be the most virtuous among mothers. According to her, I also was the most virtuous among babies, in that I never cried. She said that when I was a baby, I would wake up, play with my toys, eat well, play again and go back to sleep. When I recall that our second of three daughters cried only about three times, and that was when she had good reason to do so, I can come close to believing that my mother was sincere in what she remembered about me.

I do recall, however, a time when I cried some years later, after I had graduated from the baby crib, and after having gone through the toddler period.

I was the only member of the family who had a private bed. It was a cot, and I really enjoyed it. I sometimes wonder if it was the only good cot in town.

Apparently, my parents gave permission to loan my bed to some men to use for carrying a man out of the deep forest; there, of course, were no paramedics or medical clinics in town. The man being carried must have been far in the woods. The worst day in my life thus far was upon me. When I saw my bed missing, I was emotionally distraught and cried without stopping for hour after hour. I would repeatedly run to the door, grab the door knob time and time again, wondering why the men did not come back with my bed. I do not recall stopping crying.

I missed my cot early in the morning, and it did not come back until late in the afternoon. I can imagine I received a great sense of pleasure and feeling of security that night when I laid my head down on that precious piece of property.

In 1919, the children of Fairbanks never felt unpainted buildings were anything unusual. Only a few of these children's names are remembered by the author today. In the front row: Third from left is Gladys Anderson, fifth is Delima Clapperton, sixth is John Lauerer, seventh is Joe Lauerer, and ninth from left is Katherine Lauerer. None of the children in the back row are identified. The building in the background on the right is the mill's office building.

CHAPTER 3

Simple Pleasures

My parents had two cows that were the only source of milk for the town. I helped deliver the raw milk to the various homes in town. The two cows furnished enough milk for all of them and there still was plenty for our home. There were no other cows to contaminate ours. The only time our cows saw other cattle was when we walked them six miles for breeding.

I delivered milk to the various homes in cleaned lard cans that had good handles, since no such item as a milk bottle was ever seen in those days. The present laws of sanitation, sterilization and pasteurization were no doubt non-existent, at least for small pioneer towns. Maybe they were not needed.

There also was not much need for medication or doctoring. I recall a doctor coming to town when my sister was born. The next time was about 10 years later. Our neighbor was such a poor shot that he only wounded his wife when he tried to kill her suspected boyfriend. My folks showed their bravery when they went over to the neighbor's wife to try to help her until a doctor finally arrived from Two Harbors.

I recall one time my father ordered a hog from Duluth. He got the carcass and spent a long evening cutting up the animal. He did the work at night by a kerosene lantern, so apparently was not able to examine the meat closely. We had our first meal the following day. I believe I was the first one in the family to find the meat was not fit for human consumption. It was full of boils! There were pockets of some kind of black fluid that looked like dirty motor oil. None of us was brave enough to put any of the pieces into our mouths. All the meat was repacked and returned to Duluth. I wish I could show people today the government inspection stamps so clearly marked all

15

over the meat. As I remember, the stamps read something like "Inspected and approved by the U.S. Dept. of Agriculture."

One day, while looking for something to do, I saw a one-legged man with only one crutch unloading a railroad boxcar of horses right near our cabin. He must have unloaded at least eight or 10 horses. With amazing dexterity, he was able to jump-mount the various teams and ride them in line so later he could drive them to Smith's Headquarters logging camp. He was able to mount and dismount with the greatest of ease, but I'll never know why he didn't ride one of the animals when he led them up to Smith's camp. Instead, he walked, using his crutch, all three-quarters of a mile out to the logging camp. The weather was cold and frosty and I could hear his crutch making a grinding, crunching and sometimes squeaking noise in the hardened snow. Finally, as the stars came out, the noise stopped and I knew that the horses were at the end of their journey and in a warm barn.

There was another interesting one-legged man around town. This man had a peg leg. He must have made a living cutting pulp. He had his shack about a block from Smith's Headquarters camp. He was not part of the camp, and in fact had nothing to do with it. He lived there long after the camp was closed. How this man got along with his disability is a puzzle. He, along with his wife and child, lived in the poorest shack I have ever seen. The shack was made of one-inch rough-cut boards. All there was for insulation was newspaper pages.

It seems the snow in those years was much heavier than today, and still not a big problem. The solution in those days was not to stay inside and listen to the radio or watch the television. The big snow drifts froze hard and enabled us to make excellent snow bricks that made it easy to make snow houses, which we did for a number of years. The only things we needed that nature did not provide were a few two-by-fours to serve as rafters. We would build fires in the snow houses and roast marshmallows. The fires, of course, were small and had to be watched constantly.

Every winter, we shoveled an area on Lake Cadotte so we could play hockey. Even on cold Saturday nights when the temperature was just above zero, we skated while people drove off to the country dances. I recall that we would sometimes still be out there skating when the dancers returned after midnight. The air in Fairbanks was so clean that the stars and the northern lights, particularly in winter, were really something to enjoy.

One year, Lake Cadotte froze hard before snow came and we could skate the full two miles to the northern shore and the full half mile width. At night, the clean ice looked like water. I don't recall whether we informed our parents or asked permission.

One night, when the three of us were saying our prayers out loud and in unison, my dad happened to open the front door and saw that the huge barn on the hill near the sawmill was on fire. The barn, which held 20 horses, really made a sight all in flames. People told us the next day that many horses were running free with their backs on fire. I imagine their tails and manes were on fire also. Two burned horses did not die, but probably should have for their own good.

The dear pioneer cabin in which I was raised was a perfect fire trap. The roof was made of untreated tinder-dry cedar shin-

The Lauerer cabin. (left to right) John, Theresa, Katherine, Joseph, Joe

17

gles. The stove pipe went almost straight up. The stove was one of those so-called "airtight" heaters made of thin sheet metal that I never considered very safe. They never had grates. Our cabin roof caught fire two times. I never saw the first fire. I can only assume the shingles caught fire because there was a patch on the roof with brand new shingles near the outside stove pipe. I did see the second fire, which was fortunately at the peak of the roof and confined to the shingles. This second fire was extinguished with pails of water. I believe a train happened to be in the station and that the train men helped to save the cabin. The pump near our home was kept in repair by the railroad, I believe, so the crews could get good, cold drinking water.

After the fire, Dad had a safe, brick chimney installed. Also, a better and safer heater was installed, different than the first one I recall seeing. The stove might have been changed before the fire or after, I can't really remember. The chimney went five feet outside the roof and had a top to make it safe.

Sometimes when a fire in the stove was hard to keep burning, dad would throw some kerosene on it. This really made the stove shudder.

We had a chicken coop. One time, some friends left town. They asked us to "kitty sit" their two cats. Apparently it was decided to keep the two cats in the chicken coop with about 25 chickens and one of those old upright kerosene heaters. That night, a train man stopped at the pump about a half block from our house to get drinking water to have in the caboose. Even though it was late, my father was wide awake. Father made extra money by being a security guard and a night watchman whose job it was to watch for fire in the lumberyard. The train man came to our cabin and told dad we had a building afire in the back. What a sight to see those chickens cooked with all their feathers on and two cats among them! The cats must have played with each other and tipped the heater over.

One other fire I remember was a home on the extreme west of the row of houses on the hill overlooking the sawmill. All I saw of this fire was the smoke and pieces of drifting tar paper.

The most available and dependable items for transportation were feet. There were no cars or busses, and I recall seeing only one buggy. There were hardly any playthings. Yet, in this bleak environment, I was neither bored nor lonely. Why should I be? I captured as "mine" anything that moved, ran or hauled. I spent hours watching the trains on the double tracks and in the big switching yard, which was in plain view from the slight hill on which my home stood. Steam haulers and sawmills were also some of my favorite items to enjoy. Even the smoke from the three large smokestacks and the screen top — the smoke during the day and the sparks at night — held my attention.

During these years, my dad worked every day in the sawmill when it was running and in the lumberyard in the winter. He worked a lot of overtime. He never abused alcohol and never gambled. Still, he never bought any toys for me. When I wanted to play train, I remember rolling cans that had food in them and pretending they were railway cars being pushed around.

In later years, when I played in our yard overlooking the rail yards, I created sort of a mirage in childhood fantasy. In my mind I imagined particularly that the locomotive or engine of the train, with it's puffing smoke, hissing steam, it's ringing bell and whistle could really be a living, powerful entity. This was easy to do, particularly with the engines of freight trains, as they did all the switching work in assembling and making up of trains. When engines acted so lifelike in doing their humping to rearrange the cars into the desired order before the train left Fairbanks, in my young brain, I thought the engine liked certain cars more and disliked others. Even an adult who spends time watching the humping procedure when switching is done to make up a new train can get some fun out of this. I played this game because I had so few others around to play with and had to keep myself occupied.

If I would have been able to engage in little league sports and play in a crowded, normal play yard with many children, I would not have had to resort to such fantasies. I had the same kind of fantasy with steam haulers, which to a young child looked and acted much as a railroad steam engine, only they ran and hauled large sleighs of logs.

When I was a boy, nothing gave me a more powerful feeling than to know I could do just what I wanted to do. The railroad station in Fairbanks was a main stopping place for unloading cargo and people, and all passenger trains stopped there. But most of the settlements in the surrounding area were flag stations. This meant that the big passenger trains did not stop there unless someone flagged them down in order to get a ride.

On cold, starry nights, when I wanted to stop one of these long passenger trains, the only tool I needed was a kerosene lantern or a flashlight. I would swing my light from left to right pointed at the train's locomotive in front of me.

Quickly, I would get a reply. "Toot, toot!" Then the brakes would screech, sparks would fly off the big drive wheels, and the train would start to slow down. How the engineer could control the train so the front of the third coach stopped where I was waiting, I will never know. A neatly dressed man with an attractive blue military captain's cap opened the door in the front of the coach. He carried a large, heavy metal stepstool in his right hand and had no difficulty in the cold, dark night to make the long step down to the ground and place the stool so I could board the train.

I often used this method to stop a train and travel where I needed or wanted to go in the North Woods. One place I enjoyed going was a flag station named Reno, three miles north of Fairbanks. Fairbanks had mostly German people in it and the Skibo mill area was heavily laden with Swedish and Finnish people. Reno was populated by one French family named LaLonde.

The LaLonde boys loved to hunt while logging and they had a bull that was trained to pull a loaded sleigh. What a way to solve a transportation problem! They often carried loaded guns and shot grouse from the top of the sleigh.

Their resourcefulness and determination in the face of a difficult task proved helpful in solving a veterinary problem for my daddy once. After giving birth, one of our cows could not get up. The LaLonde boys cut a hole in the roof of the barn, put a big strap under the cow's belly, and operating through the roof, they jacked her up into a standing position with the chain block. After a vinegar tonic and a massage to her legs, she recovered.

Adjusting to America and the remote Fairbanks world was difficult for my parents. My mother never showed her longings for the old country, perhaps because her sister, Katherine Huber, lived nearby. The large Huber family acted as our sponsors when we came to America, and they made our family's adjustment to American food, language and culture easier. They helped us socially and in other ways, and visiting with our dear cousins was an activity that I anticipated with eagerness each day.

Dad, on the other hand, so missed the singing, music and dancing of the happy people in Bavaria, that he talked about it at least once a week. I was afraid he needed to cry to unload his feelings. Good music was hard to come by in this white pine forest. The few holidays each year when we attended a dance only seemed to rekindle his need for some of that Bavarian pleasure. He would talk of his beloved Bavarian music and often cranked up our old Victor phonograph to play those records that gave him the relief he so much needed. He gained strength by having us children dance with him and Mother right there in our home.

Dad enjoyed his work with his friends in the sawmill, and the fulfillment he gained from seeing what he could do with every piece of wood he touched, helped cure his loneliness. Eventually, these simple pleasures helped him adjust to life in America.

I Remember Fairbanks and Skibo

CHAPTER 4

Sawmill Symphonies

My dad worked in the noisy, wonderful sawmill as a tail sawyer next to the sawyer. The sawyer really ran the mill because he controlled the carriages that ran back and forth and enabled the huge band saw to rip the boards off the logs which the carriage held in its grip. The mill gave us the money for living, and at the same time, gave my father a job he liked ever so much. I am sure that Dad and his co-workers enjoyed themselves immensely. The men seemed to enjoy every aspect of the environment — the noise, the flying sawdust, the hissing steam, and the feel of the sawed wood.

My dad worked in the exact center of the mill and had the pleasure of handling every piece of manufactured wood that

The sawmill at Fairbanks with the three smokestacks at the right and the waste burner to the left. Cadotte Lake is behind the mill.

23

came off every log that traveled up the sluice into the mill. With his big mitt-covered hands or short cant hook, my daddy handled every board, beam, bark or slab, and decided which was waste wood to be guided to the huge burner and which was good lumber destined to become part of homes in eastern cities or St. Louis.

I spent ever so much time sitting on the observation platform, from which I could oversee much of the mill's operation. When one has observed the operation of the large steam-powered mill run by hands and minds of men, one marvels at the various functions — rolling the logs, turning them, sending the good lumber to storage and the bark and imperfect planks on their way as discards. The carriage that held the logs went back and forth so close to me!

Many of the workers could see me, and they would engage in much pantomime because, of course, they would have no success in trying to say anything due to the deafening noise. Smiling, pointing, waving and pantomiming was good enough for me to communicate with my daddy. I enjoyed every moment I spent in that building. There were so few guards. Today's factories would have so many guards, fences and other protective devices. Our hundreds of lawyers and lawsuits do ruin much of the living in this world.

I never was in the mill when it was idle, such as before the start, when it stopped for the noon hour, or at day's end. There also was a shutdown when the bandsaws had to be replaced because a saw was getting dull and a newly-sharpened saw had to be mounted on the wheels. I suppose it was during such moments when my dad learned most of his English.

How my dad completed his knowledge of the English language in such a noisy environment, I will never be able to figure out. The loudest noise came from the logs being forced against the large bandsaw which forced a ripping action to rip off the boards from the log. My dad could not have been more than about three feet from this saw and the terrible screech when logs were pushed into its humming blade. The screaming, thumping logs did not seem to affect my dad's hearing the least bit.

All of the noises proved just how vitally alive the steam,

wheels, belts, gears and whistles in that dear old sawmill were. The only thing I could not figure out was how the thin membranes of my daddy's eardrums could still catch every sound coming from my mother's voice when he came home after eight hours of work. He married the most gentle and soft-spoken German woman I ever heard.

One would think that the workmen would get tired and that accidents would result. I never learned of any serious accident in the mill, the lumberyard, the hauling of lumber or the unloading of logs from railroad cars where the logs rolled off the flat cars and splashed into the lake or crashed onto the ice. I always considered this last a rather dangerous job, as the logging chains were uncoupled allowing the logs to explode loose and fall off the railroad cars that were parked on the trestle for unloading.

I have decided that the men working in this mill were so full of smiles and never seemed bored with work or life because their effort was so productive; that every man had a good feeling because he could see what happened to the logs, to the boards, and even to the bark slabs that were sent his way. I believe that when workers see the results of their endeavor — the day's work resulting from their minds and hands and their skilled use of tools — the day's work is not stressful.

I clearly recall that the mill was still running full speed ahead on Armistice Day, when World War I ended on November 11, 1918. I am glad I was not aware of the day the mill closed in 1922 or 1923. It must have been sad when the last log rolled off the holding floor onto the carriage, when the hissing steam breathed its last; when the gears and cogs and pulleys made their last turn; and then the shrill whistle from the mill marked the end of an era in Fairbanks.

I was not present when the Fairbanks sawmill was built, but I witnessed its death. In fact, I helped load the last boxcar load of lumber. The mill was dismembered and I helped load the machinery onto a flat railroad car at the same loading dock where the railroad boxcar of lumber was loaded.

Dad was out of work. The only place where he found work was on the railroad section gang. I can remember the adjustment he had to make to, what was for him, such a monotonous and boring way to support himself and his family. Although the work was out in the fresh air and sunshine, he told us again and again how long the day took to pass. This boredom lasted months. However, there was hardly another way to get a steady-paying job in the area, and this was the only way to support the family. Finally, he adjusted. At least he quit complaining. He ended up working long enough to retire and get a pension.

I remember so clearly the years of waking up early in the morning in that cabin in Fairbanks. For some reason, I remember only waking up in the wintertime and not so much the summertime, perhaps because summer mornings weren't as impressive. In the winter, my father's boots would make noises on the snow as he walked by my window carrying water from the town pump to the kitchen for Mother and to the barn for the cows. Such a variety of sounds came from his soles and heels. Sometimes there was a grinding sound, then a squeak or a squeal. Often there was a thud. Later in the morning, I would hear him tending to the wood fire in the stove.

The burning wick of the kerosene lamp cast enough light into my bedroom on those dark winter mornings that I could see my father enjoying his breakfast. For years he seemed content to survive on buttered rye bread and coffee breakfasts. After such a lean meal, he would work at hard labor. Still, he kept a good strong body and lived to the age of 72. He ate much cabbage in the form of sauerkraut. I can still see him stamping on ground cabbage in a barrel with his feet in stockings. He did make good sauerkraut.

We tightly closed the windows and doors of our humble log cabin to make survival possible during the long, bitter winter nights, but one morning I woke up and my curiosity somehow sensed that something was going on outside. The way "Old Man Winter" was growling around the corners of our cozy cabin, I certainly did not want to open a door or window and let the monster inside. Because our cabin had only single glass panes, all our windows had a very heavy coating of frost. However, nature had provided me with the necessary tools, and with my fingernails and breath, I could make a peephole.

The second Lauerer home, about 1921 or 1922. It is one of only two buildings still standing from the original Fairbanks settlement. The only change to this home is that it has been painted. The other building has been remodeled, making the Lauerer home the only building that remains in its original state today.

With persistence and patience, my fingernails and maybe my breath, I very soon had a sighting on my world out there. And what a sight it was! A slow-moving, black object was making headway through the deep white snow in the open field outside my window; there was no road or trail. The machine was releasing puffs of dark smoke which kept time with the noise of drive pistons being driven by steam and making the machine travel.

Steam haulers needed no rails, pavement, blacktop or gravel roads. The smoking machines traveled exclusively in frozen and snow-covered swamps and river bottoms, up frozen roads to the logging areas. They avoided hills when possible, not only because it was difficult to haul loads up the hill, but also to haul them down. Because many of the roads were icy on the downhill areas, hay was spread on the roads to assist these machines, which had no brakes, to control the pull of gravity.

Steam haulers were the marvel of the white pine logging world. These machines normally hauled a rather long train of

Steam haulers were used widely in northern Minnesota logging camps during the early part of the century.

huge sleds — each sled held about a railroad car of logs. Many of these sleds were parked in town. When the Smith's Headquarters camp operation died, several of these sleds were parked in the acreage between my cabin home and my school, not far from the boardwalk that led from the town pump and past our cabin on toward the school. These sleds made ideal climbing items for little boys to crawl and play on.

Our favorite subjects to draw on the blackboards in school were not houses, trains, locomotives or cars, but the steam haulers. I don't know why, but only the boys enjoyed drawing them. The one who could draw the largest and most impressive machine was the most admired.

I am so glad I have a number of large framed photographs of the steam haulers that operated not only in the Fairbanks mill area and the Smith's Headquarters camp area, but also in Skibo and the Skibo mill area. I do not agree with a write-up that appeared in the Minneapolis newspaper some years ago claiming these machines were a failure throughout Minnesota and northern Wisconsin. They certainly were a success in the Fairbanks and Skibo area. My framed pictures testify to that.

CHAPTER 5

One-room Schoolhouse

The one-room white school sat on the hill overlooking the town and my cabin home, which was closer than the rest of the town. The school was at the extreme northern end of the clearing made for the town. There was a special block-like clearing fenced in just for the school.

The Fairbanks school as it appeared before the addition of the porch and replacement of the windows. The first person at the left is Orville Craven, next is Clifford Craven, and sixth is Mary Huber. Other students are unknown. Many days during those years, attendance in this one-room school was only 17.

The two-story bar and hotel was located in the extreme southern border, again, almost in the forest, but in addition, one could say it was just about in a dismal, very soft swamp.

There was a law — one of the very few there were to obey (and that was obeyed) — that required this extreme space between the enjoying adult men and their serious studying children. You see, whoever wanted the saloon did not want the children seeing their fathers having a good time with the mill hands and lumberjacks and liquor.

Students at Fairbanks School. Front Row (left to right): Nora Anderson, Delima Clapperton, Lydia Craven, John Lauerer, Gladys Anderson; Second Row: Claude Burbey, Sulo Beck, Clifford Craven, Eva Maki, Joe Lauerer; Back Row: Peter Ludgate (at left standing on railing), Lillian Gardner, Esther Craven, May Craven, ?, ?, Fred Mower (at right on railing).

There was a very well-kept boardwalk to the Lauerer's cabin (Imagine that! To the only residence that apparently deserved one!) from the town pump, which was the main source of drinking water. About halfway between the pump and our home, a "T" was run-off going north for about a block to the school.

The school building and the railroad track near it served other purposes than education. The large double track was sometimes used as a race track, and the depot agent would lead the way. I recall the hollering and screaming and what fun the women had at these foot races. The school building was used

The Lauerer children dressed for First Communion (left to right): Katherine, 7; John, 9; and Joe, 11.

for political meetings, and it was the only place where dances were held. I can still remember my first dance, how the men held the women and the couples twirled around the floor. The piece I remember being danced to the most was "Beautiful Ohio."

Catholic Church masses were also held in the school. I can still remember my first confessions. They were held in the girls' cloak room. That room served as the confessional where I received absolution from the priest for those awful mortal sins. There, as a young boy who tried to be good with little success, I unloaded my sins so I would be lighter to go up to heaven.

I had an uncle and aunt who refused to attend mass in the school building because they felt that worshiping in such a sinful place where those terrible dances were held would not be in God's favor.

The teachers in the school had much respect among the town's people, particularly among the families with children. Teachers had a major impact on people adjusting from the somewhat confining life inside the home to what there was outside in the real world. I will never forget the affect my first teacher had on my fears, my mind in general, and my start in adjusting to the world outside my home and the large family of relatives I spent time with on the second floor of the general store. The importance this first teacher, and some that followed, had in making me into the man I eventually became can never be over-emphasized.

On my first day at school, my mother did not walk me to school, for she could not speak English. Hardly could I. My big eyes must have indicated fear as I looked at the other 17 pupils in attendance that day. I had only seen one before.

The teacher picked me up in front of the whole school. I remember her personality being as warm as her breast as she smiled and cuddled me. For the time being, she might have taken the place of my mother, whom I was so in need of at the moment. I believe I was close to being five years old. That human being who took me in her lap served as the needed catapult to face the scary days ahead. Those days, in the pioneer towns, beginners did not start school with half days. This was the fist day I survived an entire day without my mother. The fact that I started school at such an early age merely demonstrates how little control there was in those days concerning such matters.

One reason I was enrolled in school a year early was because I was so lonesome for my brother, Joe, who was a year and a half older than me. I so much missed him that I was a problem at home. However, being away from my mother and not being able to run to my several relatives of whom I was very fond made my first days at school difficult, even though Joe was there. I couldn't play or be with him when school was in session. Still, the fact that he was in the same room with me helped. Joe's first days in school must have been even harder than mine. He must have known even less English than I, and did not have an older member of the family in the school room to give him extra security.

How I could finish learning English and still get such a good start on my grade school education, I cannot understand. My English vocabulary was almost nil. Yet, in just a few years, I was asked to skip the sixth grade. What little bit of English I knew in the beginning, I learned from Joe; and I give him much credit for my success in school.

Nothing interests me more than to read about and listen to reasons why European and Japanese people do a better job teaching their young than the best schools of our nation. I think of the wonderful buildings we have and the great facilities available, how well-trained our teachers seem to be; and of all the books, televisions, computers, tapes, projectors and other tools our modern schools have. All these items to impart and sustain knowledge seem to be of little consequence if we are to believe what our "smart" critics tell us. We are told every so often that when we test our children they just do not measure up.

When I think about our one-room school, I could easily get myself into a quandary, so I try to quickly change my thinking subject. To any "doubtin' Thomas" I can say, "At least I received a super education in that dear one-room school at Fairbanks."

Those who never attended a one-room school in the forest

Students in the one-room school at Fairbanks. Left to right seated, Gladys Anderson, John Lauerer (wearing striped shirt and tie), Marjorie Smith, Delima Clapperton (wearing white dress, front center), ?, Clifford Craven (reading book, front right); Left to right standing, May Craven, Eva Maki, ?, Joe Lauerer (with tie), Darlene Courtier.

may not know what a school without electric power is like. I had to share one book and one seat with another student part of the time one year. If someone takes this lightly, that individual should try studying printed pages with another person. It must have been hard for one teacher to teach all subjects every day.

That first teacher must have really made me shift into high gear. I took off like a fire engine, making unbelievable progress learning English, reading, writing, arithmetic and geography. In a way, it was fun accepting new information every day as another challenge. When my first teacher left, another one came. Of course, there were no longer any more laps to sit on. I was now too big anyway, and some teachers were too mean, so I would probably have refused had I been young enough.

One teacher who qualified under the "mean" category actually, today, would qualify for court action and lawsuit for doling out cruel punishment. She must have considered me to be the worst student in class because she never treated another kid as she did me. Because I was sharing a book with another boy, I of course whispered to the boy. She saw me, so on my birthday she sentenced me to the wall behind the furnace. What a way to celebrate my birthday! All day I could not sit, walk or lie down. I do not recall telling of this terrible treatment to my parents. Maybe it was always the custom in those days to not report punishment at school for fear of having it duplicated at home.

I recall a teacher who was going to slap my hands and also the hands of another student. As I recall, the other terrible offender was slapped first. When it was my turn and I was told to stretch out my hands, I stuck both hands in my pockets so firmly they never got slapped. She did not place her hands in my pockets to pull the hands out. I doubt she held off for fear of sexual harassment charges or child abuse charges, for those were unknown quandaries in that world. In fact, there was one incident when a principal grabbed a boy by the shoulders and shook him violently. Today, those actions would probably result in lawsuits, but never in the days when I was young.

I would not have a complete history of our small pioneer town without reporting on the only man teacher I had in the one-room school. He was a tough, old, Irish schoolmaster who taught us during my last four years. One event, which took place at the most anticipated part of the Christmas season, shows he was somewhat harder on boys than girls.

Actually, I also give part of the credit, or blame, for ruining the school Christmas program to the Kaiser. Most people familiar with European history know that young men who spent years in Adolf Hitler's army carried with them certain attributes that affected their behavior until death. Two of these are, "never accept defeat" and "always fight to gain the most." My dad was in the Kaiser's army, so our household was run with firmness in all ways and all times.

Because I was in the top grade, this Irish teacher gave me heavy parts in plays. During one of our rehearsals, my brother and another boy were engaging in some horseplay in which the other boy fell down. The schoolmaster decided the proper punishment was to kick both boys out of the program.

When this was reported at home, the response from the

head of our household was immediate, firm and resolute. When I reported that I was being used to fill the void in the various plays, the response was not negotiable. I was ordered to study hard and take part in the revised rehearsals, but when the final night arrived for the program to present the performance, I would not be allowed to go. I would be ordered to stay at home.

This was quite a hard strain to learn additional parts while knowing full-well the whole thing was of no avail. Days passed. We practiced. The final night before Christmas vacation came closer and closer. With a lump in my throat, I realized tonight was the night. As night came, the stars came out. I heard conversation in the distance getting louder. Then laughter could be heard. The citizens of Fairbanks were walking up to the school via the boardwalk close to our house. People were so happy thinking forward to the great evening, to the music and the acting in the plays. People were talking in such an excited mood.

As the Coleman gasoline lights were casting their rays across the landscape onto the snowdrifts, the last word on the sidewalk outside our cabin was heard. Now Dad spoke up, "Now you and I will walk up to the school, you will go in the school and tell Mr. O'Brien that you are not coming in tonight, and why."

What a walk! What a messenger of sad tidings! So many times since I was almost five years old I had walked and run with a light heart. A sad and heavy walk this was. Normally, I walked with my eyes to the heavens, looking for the Aurora Borealis. Not this night. It was cold. The snow sparkled in the moonlight while, I imagine, the stars twinkled above. My poor heart thumped as I saw O'Brien looking out the window for one certain boy. I almost hoped the sidewalk would go on forever and that my walk would never end.

Finally, it did end. I got to the steps and was able to lift up one foot. Then, I hesitated. The next foot for the second step seemed so heavy. I fearfully told Dad that I just could not go on. I felt very glad that the hook with Dad's razor strop was not within reach.

Believe it or not, no word was said on our walk back down

Fairbanks School after the porch was added to the front

to our cabin. No word was said to me anywhere in town. Also no word was said about this evening that I so successfully and completely ruined when the teacher came back to school at the restarting of classes after Christmas vacation. I was tending to the furnace when the teacher came into the room. He greeted me and while wiping his hands said, "It's pretty cold this morning."

Normally, on this night, every student gets some gift besides nuts and candy. I cannot recall how bleak our home must have been without either and how the people must have felt and what they talked about as they walked by the Lauerer's cabin on their way back down from the school to their homes.

When my brother and I went to school in Aurora, the "smart" people in Fairbanks warned us that we would be initiated and abused as strange boys before being accepted. A day or two before school started, two of the most popular boys in the school and who were also to be in our class, did us a big favor. They gave us a thorough tour of the entire school. They showed us the first swimming pool, the first gym and the first auditorium we had ever seen, as well as our classrooms. These boys were "it." They were good-looking and excellent athletes.

They were popular with the girls and had all the girls they wanted, for as long as they wanted. Because these two boys treated us as close friends, the other boys saw that we were not strangers entirely. How could anyone think we needed to be initiated? We were accepted immediately as the closest of friends. I studied printing as one of my classes and helped produce the school newspaper, the **Aurora Borealis**.

Fairbanks baseball team, also known as the Colvin-Robb Sawmill team. Front row: fifth man from left, George Huber; Back row (left to right): Pratten, Doan, Hoffman, Leo LaLonde (pitcher), Piper, Smith and Herrick.

CHAPTER 6

Swift and Silent Justice

When I was part of Fairbanks, people could live for over a decade without lawyers, courts and judges. We have to give credit where credit is due. However, some sections of Fairbanks' history are not easy to relate to others. As the world turns, and as people act and react, the worst sometimes do harm to the best.

One family that was harmed was, in my judgment, the best. The mother did the most unselfish good in the community. The father had important responsibility in the sawmill's operations, although I do not think he had much to do with the mechanical end of the operation. A newly-arrived family brought with it what might be termed a "bad" boy. I was told that this boy either raped, or tried to rape, one of the very nice daughters of the nice family mentioned above. The girl told her daddy and immediately, justice was carried out by her daddy!

I viewed a portion of that justice. I saw the girl's daddy walking rather briskly down from school where he had captured the criminal. He had a big club in his hand. It reminded me of the killing clubs the caveman used for getting meat in the forest and for killing his enemy. The girl's daddy was apparently walking his captive to the woodshed at home. The school had a good woodshed. I do not know why that was not used. Maybe because there was no wood in it, only coal.

One day, a boy in our school became sick and had to go to the outdoor toilet very urgently. He raised his hand for permission to leave the room. Mr. O'Brien refused. The boy finally got up and rushed out of the school. The poor kid really had a bad case of diarrhea. He must have run out of toilet paper because the white painted walls showed that he tried to clean his soiled fingers from the diarrheic by wiping both hands on the wall.

Why nobody became concerned enough about those terribly soiled walls, I just don't know, but the schoolmaster who really may have caused the terrible sight got his eyes full. With the way I have reacted to most things that needed doing in this environment of mine, I don't know why I didn't wash the wall.

There was one other set of marks in our town that was never removed, and I don't know why. Of course, to do that might have entailed a covering with new tar paper. The girl who was harmed by the bad boy did something most unusual. This girl was one of two in school who had a crush on me. All but one of the pictures I have from those years show her by my side, but I never touched her. At this stage, I would only touch a girl if I danced with her, and I was too young for even that.

In a puppy love mood, she let her artistic skill go too far. In the home where she lived, only the back portion, which was the kitchen part, was covered with tar paper. She wrote notes to me of a puppy love nature with white chalk.

Again, this was another subject that never was talked about. Why was this mess not removed by her parents? And why didn't someone talk? I believe the sawmill would have furnished new tar paper to such an important family.

CHAPTER 7

Out Behind the Barn

Sex education left quite a bit to be desired. As a young boy, I was told that when a cow mates with a bull, she simply looks at the bull and then she will get a calf. Nothing more was said, not even when a beautiful calf came into the world. This lack of talking about sex is a good example of Bavarian culture and how those Germans raised and educated their little boys. Maybe they believed that alleys could take over such education. Unfortunately, there were no alleys in Fairbanks.

As far as sex education for little boys in homes or in the one room in Fairbanks' school, there was nothing except a few lies. Of course, how could one discuss sex with third and fourth graders when boys starting pubic development, like the seventh and eighth graders, were in the same room?

I was told that modesty meant not displaying one's body. Apparently, if little boys always kept certain organs hidden and never let anyone, not even themselves, see them, there would never be a problem later in life. One boy in town was even told by a Catholic priest that he must never look at his private parts. I wonder if this boy was also told a violation would prevent him from getting into heaven?

My knowledge of sex was not increased in my home, where the normal sex act was never discussed. I was told that a certain aunt of mine would cut off any exposed private parts if they were allowed to be seen on one's body bare. This made a very big impression on me and was carefully avoided. I believed the story so strongly that once when Dad had cut many long birch logs with lots of branches, I pretended I had a knife and cut off the imaginary private parts from the crotch of the trees. Meanwhile, my relationship with that dear aunt was

41

nothing but the best. For many years, I admired a picture of myself sitting on my aunt's lap.

While still a boy, I helped my dad drive a cow six miles into the forest to "mate" with a bull. I had to assist because it took two people to make the cow walk steadily, one person leading with a rope fastened at the cow's head and another person walking close behind near the animal's tail. My brother Joe was away at school and I had not yet begun to attend. The wagon trail we took was very bad for walking because it was spring; the trail was flooded and there were many wagon-wheel ruts and rocks, as well as one terribly high hill we had to climb. There were many side roads and a few curves which were necessary because the trail had to go between two lakes. Highway 16 today follows this same route.

The first hour or so of our trip was pretty boring. No animals or birds of any kind were to be seen. After a while, a team of horses pulling a wagon came up behind us. The big wheels, big spokes and iron rims made a pretty sight as the four of them revolved in unison. I had never had the pleasure of riding on one of the big wagons that hauled lumber, boxes, barrels, groceries and such, or of sitting on one of those good seats with springs. Because the trip was so hard, or maybe because he thought I would enjoy the ride, Dad asked the driver if I could have a ride. The wheels were so big that the wagon had no trouble going over the rocks, down the ruts and out of the holes, so the rest of the trip out to the "mating" was really pleasurable.

My father and I, however, had to part for a time. No way could he watch me see the first sexual performance of my life. It would have hurt him as much to watch me as he felt it would have hurt me to see that rough, mad-looking, big bull "attack" that dear, lovely heifer. All the more so because the heifer was trapped in a "sex cage" from which there was no escape until the bull had completed his task.

As so often happens with parents, Dad planned to divert me with candy. He gave me money and sent me to the store, but failed to emphasize enough that I was to absolutely wait there until he and the cow came to pick me up. Away I went.

When I walked out of the store with my bag of candy, I

was looking for my dear heifer, which unknown to me was probably no longer a virgin. I didn't think the cow would have to look at the bull long, just a glance should be enough to get her pregnant. After waiting for quite a while, I began to feel alone and lost. I remembered the wolves around our cabin and worried that maybe a wolf had gotten our cow.

I began to be frightened. It was six miles back down the muddy trail to home. I remembered that all the side roads had been on the right hand side coming out from town, and that Dad had ignored all the side roads. I remembered that the second half of the trip had been almost a straight trail, after that mountain which was almost like a cliff to go up. I started out for home.

At the pinnacle of the cliff I saw what appeared to be sparkling blue diamonds in the distance. It was Lake Cadotte! I was only a mile from home. Before I went too much further, a fierce looking animal approached me. I was sure it was a wolf, so I ran, and spilled some of my candy. Later, my dad told me how happy it made him to see that candy and how glad it made him to know I beat him and the cow home. Dad said that after

Joseph Lauerer tends to the Lauerer family's cows in the pasture behind Fairbanks School.

43

the cow and the bull had seen enough of each other, he had stopped at the store to pick me up. He asked where I was and the storekeeper told him I had said, "I AM GOING TO FAIR-BANKS."

When I was about 14 years old, Dad assigned me the breeding duty. He requested that I take our beautiful young virgin heifer to a farm that was strange to me. When I and my virgin arrived there, only a beautiful young lady was home. I sure was glad that she had one of those cow cages with only one entrance at the front and no other escape. We both watched the performance with very little conversation, and after paying for the sex, the heifer and I walked home. This was my sex education.

CHAPTER 8

Rails for Work and Play

Skibo was a railroad station and logging area north of Fairbanks. It's where I worked five summers at hard labor to earn cash so I could finish high school and go to college. Skibo was almost as important to my life as Fairbanks, even though it was wilder. Skibo was also important as far as timber history is concerned.

There was a three-mile railroad spur running not far from the St. Louis River east of Skibo, to the Skibo mill. At Skibo mill, there was a dam with locks to control the water for floating timber down to the mill. Skibo did not have wagon trails like Fairbanks, so Skibo could be considered as being landlocked except for the railroad. Skibo was nine miles from Fairbanks by railroad. For this reason, there was some knowledge and relationship between the people of the two towns.

When I think of my days in Skibo, I try to figure out why in the world there were eight hermits living one to five miles out in the wilderness surrounding Skibo. Fairbanks had no hermits living in the surrounding forests and yet, in Skibo, there were eight. These were nice, well-adjusted men, somewhat educated, dressed properly, and normal to talk to. The only thing a bit different about them was the fact that they never got married or had much to do with women, with one exception — one of the eight got married late in life to a woman who left her husband. I considered most of these men as friends.

I have marked on a sketch the approximate locations where five of these men lived around Skibo. I do not know where the other men lived. Bert Jones and Ralph Andrews were professional trappers and I have never been in, or seen, any of the places where they lived. I do know they had more than one cabin or shack. Louis Turnquist also had two cabins. These

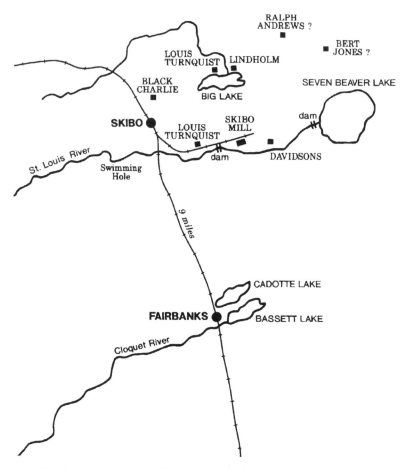

men had very long trap lines and during the season when days were very short, they needed cabins or shacks in far-off extended areas. They could not consume precious daylight hours backtracking over the same territory for home.

Some of the hermits worked on the railroad repair crews during the summer. The crews were temporarily enlarged in the summers because of needed extra repair due to the damage caused by 20 or more hundred-car ore trains a day.

When 15, I broke my first law by lying about my age and starting work at common labor. I was anxious to start accumulating money for education. I was familiar with hard labor and

I felt strong enough to work for the railroad. The boss liked me and always hired me when school ended and worked me until school restarted. In the spring, if his crew was full, he would take me as an extra. On two occasions, I stayed out of school a year to store money. Those years, the boss used me almost until winter. The section crews rode to work on what we called "speeders" even though they never were run very speedily. There was a hand pumping car that we were allowed to use to pump our way out on the spur the three miles to the Skibo mill. The mill was dead and torn down, but we still used the term Skibo mill.

I enjoyed the wildlife. I am referring to animals in the Skibo area. In those days, the Department of Natural Resources (DNR) did not have to kill and dispose of wounded animals hurt by fences and trains. Whenever we saw a crippled deer, our boss would stop the speeder, give me a maul and say, "Johnny, go kill that deer." I killed all wounded deer and left the carcasses to rot, as was the practice in those days.

Our section boss was a nice man. He and I developed a good friendship. He would usually give us a relief once in the morning and once in the afternoon. When he thought it was

A section crew. Sebastian Huber, crew boss, is standing on the ground.

time for a relief, he would say, "Boys, take five." Although he didn't work as hard as the crew, he got tired and sure could sleep harder. In fact, quite often he would fall sound asleep. When this happened, we lowered our conversation and finally stopped talking entirely. Sometimes he would sleep on and on. Usually after about 20 minutes he would wake with a start and say, "Oh my! I almost fell asleep." Then, back to work we'd go.

Much of the four miles we kept in repair was uphill. This meant that the hundred-car ore train would have to go slow. We didn't object to the passing trains because this gave us a longer time to legally loaf.

Many days we "raised track" because low stretches developed. I liked this because I could get away from the boring, monotonous work of "tamping ties," a tedious operation that involved forcing gravel or crushed rock underneath the ties. I don't know how, when or why, but I started carrying both the very heavy rail jack and the big lining bar that was used to pump the jack that raised the heavy rail. Raising track was usually a two-man operation requiring one man to carry each tool. Raising track not only was less boring, but it gave me great fulfillment to be strong enough to raise the railroad all alone. I enjoyed being one man raising the railroad. Another one-man job was running the speeder to look for bad rails that needed replacing, and to watch for forest fires started by the engine's exhaust and the hot cinders that would sometimes spew out.

I had a partner, a bit smaller than I, all one summer. Partners in railroad gangs do much of the work while close together, especially taking out old ties and replacing them with new ties. I have always been an easy man to get along with, and we had only one argument all summer. This argument concerned the placing of three new ties. I told my boss to get my partner straight, and he did. My partner was not mad.

Sometime later, my partner quit and left our crew. Only then did the rest of the crew talk about this man being homosexual. It seemed everybody knew this except me! The word gay was never used, but homo was. Just think, working that close together with never a clue or any remark. But that was the 1920s, not the 1990s. Obviously, our military was not the first to subscribe to a "don't ask, don't tell" policy. The practice was already in vogue in Skibo years ago.

Spending all those summers keeping that large double-track railroad in repair under the supervision of such an experienced boss gave me a closeness to all railroad tracks I see, cross or walk on. I invariably notice joints that are low, rails that aren't straight, ties that are loose or rotten, and tie plates or angle irons that are bad. I know the railroad I worked on had to be in better shape than average. The track we maintained was used by 17 to 20 trains a day. The steel on the southbound tracks was much heavier since that was the track that handled the trains loaded with the heavy ore.

The most frequently-used method of getting home while working on the section was to jump the ore trains. I would usually pick a spot where the trains ran fairly slow, like on an uphill grade. I would also pick the caboose, because jumping the last car on the train was much safer. I became rather skilled in running with the caboose and jumping on the last step. The trains would always stop at Fairbanks for water, so it was easy to dismount safely. My mother was a safety person. Neither she nor my dad objected to me jumping trains. I suppose that was partly because if I hadn't, I probably would not have gotten home for weekends.

One fall, I broke laws two times. When the boss woke me up from the bed and asked to go deer hunting with him, I obeyed. So I spent both full days doing something that was fun instead of work, but taking money under false pretenses. I did have a gun, but did not load it until the boss and I got into the woods. If someone asked what I was doing, of course, I was obeying my boss.

While working on the railroad at Skibo, I learned a very interesting fact about keeping the railroad in repair for the heavy ore traffic. The system really was unique. Almost every 10 miles or so a provision was made for two section repair crews. Because some of these locations ended up in small-town or remote areas, a boarding house was set up as a place for the men to eat and sleep. Although compared to the accommodations for men in lumber camps, these boarding houses — called section houses — along the railroads were almost castles, with some exceptions. I do not wish to be too critical, but remember, Skibo and even half of the Fairbanks area did not have electric power and both had to depend on ice houses for preserving food. One morning as we were finishing a good, big breakfast, we saw seven to eight live maggots crawling all over the top of the table. All of us rose quietly from our chairs, without a word. I do not recall any conversation out at work about this terrible experience.

One day, one of our twin beds (not mine) was out on the lawn in front of the section house. One of the men I knew was applying a small fire torch to the coil springs at both ends of the bed. There were many, many live bed bugs crawling out from the coil springs.

The management of the section was at times dictatorial. Often the landlord, who was boss in running the section, was also the boss of one of the section crews. Can you imagine requiring my brother Joe to eat at the section house and have the dollar deducted from his daily pay? He had to allow this even though we lived only a block and a half from the section house and had a mother who was a good cook and cooked for her hard-working husband and the rest of the family.

How good men like those I worked with could withhold any complaint about things like this I will never know. I do know that the level of tolerance people had in those days was much greater than people have today.

One summer, I worked on a telephone construction crew that was working in Skibo. I slept on a bunk in a Pullman railroad car parked on a sidetrack spur. Those noisy ore trains went by on the main track, probably about five feet from my bed. There were usually seven or eight trains a night, but I don't recall any waking me up.

For the most part, the young men who worked on the railroad in Skibo were not too bored after work, which ended at 4:00 p.m. There was always swimming in the St. Louis River, a mile south via the railroad. There was also canoeing on the St. Louis River. When we wanted to go far up the St. Louis River, we would raise the dam at Skibo mill so the water would allow us to pass over the rapids and up to Seven Beaver Lake. One summer, another man and I and a team of horses repaired another dam that held back some of the water coming out of the lake. We slept in a lumber camp, which had a good bed and a mattress. I am proud to say that we never ransacked this abandoned cabin, as so often happens to deserted buildings today.

One project we young fellows created and enjoyed was a watchtower. We built a scaffold on the highest point of a beautiful, high ridge so at night we could see lights from the various Range cities. This was done with no modern high-tech tools. We had only hand saws, crosscut saws, hammers, nails and trees, plus a small amount of sawed lumber. We built this tower a mile up the railroad from Skibo some distance in the forest east of the tracks. In the daytime, we could see nothing but a beautiful forest and a cranberry swamp, but after the sun set, we were rewarded tenfold. We could see the lights of Aurora, about six miles distant, along with McKinley and Biwabik. Aurora was the most exciting, because this was the summer before I was to begin attending high school there. It is too bad, but I never went up the watchtower on a frosty January night, when it would have been the best time to see the Aurora Borealis, because the northern lights are always best on cold nights.

We also built a floating dock out of railroad ties. We placed this in a wide and deep bay in the river. This dock made swimming more fun because much of the river shoreline, and also the bottom, was rocky. The dock, like the watchtower, was over a mile from town. It kept us healthy to walk so much after work, and it was pleasant walking because of the opportunity to see wildlife. Besides, the hiking gave us something to do.

It was fun just to build a campfire along the banks of the St. Louis River. Sometimes we would have a girl or two along. The girls were never touched, all we did was talk and enjoy nature.

I can clearly recall a time we pumped the hand car five miles down the railroad track to Allen Junction. It was a foolish and dangerous trip on a main track that carried steam trains with over 100 cars. The family with us had a car at Allen Junction and with it, we took a trip to the Range cities.

We played outdoor games and enjoyed a grassy lawn —

51

A friendly neighborhood football game. Front row (left to right): Coach who married Evelyn Walberg, Evelyn Walberg, Bill Walberg, Mary Walberg, (Mildred?) Walberg and John Lauerer. Back row: ? and Emmert Holmes.

the only one around — in the section-house area and bunkhouse grounds. I only slept in the bunkhouse once, all the other times I slept in the top floor of the section house. There were also times when we carried on intelligent conversations about history, politics and the constitution. I was very interested in this talk, perhaps because it did not occur every evening. We made very few sex jokes. We young men did engage in a number of athletic tricks, however.

We picked berries in the Skibo area along the railroad right-of-ways. The blueberries and strawberries were abundant in these areas. During the berry season I would often spend Thursday and Friday evenings picking berries to bring home to Mother on the weekend. In a couple of evenings, I could pick almost a pack full. Nothing could make my mother smile more than to get a bunch of berries to can for the winter. Today, of course, it is illegal to walk in the railroad right-of-way.

Once we made a trip into the wilds that I recall with the greatest pleasure. A group of us went to visit one of those hermits who was the farthest away from Skibo. Three of us boys

Friends return from a successful fishing trip. Emmert Holmes is standing on the ground to the left of the railroad handcar and Sig Holmes is standing on the ground to the right. Bill Walberg is third from the left, and a man named Harry is in the center on the handcar.

took two girls whose parents had the section house and we went with the hermit who had his cabin on the prettiest lake. We took the pump car to the Skibo mill area and then hiked four miles into the distant woods. Then, we took this man's boat and rowed another mile. Finally, we came to this man's beach which reached into the water.

This man had a very nice cabin. It was a very clean cabin with a nice, rather modern bed. The bed did us boys no good, that was for the girls. The three boys and the owner slept on the floor. I cannot recall that it was uncomfortable.

This hermit was a very intelligent man. He had no ice box, yet his food seemed to be ok. I learned that this man could preserve fish for a time by putting them deep under the moss that grew under the large pine trees. This land impressed me so that when I began buying land years later, I bought part of it. I felt so bad when I discovered this nice man's cabin had burned and he had burned with it.

There were times when I enjoyed being alone. I recall one time I pumped one of those hand cars on a railroad spur three miles to the Skibo mill area and took a canoe trip on the St. Louis River all alone. What one can experience in the quiet and solitude is great. A giant bull moose had his head and immense rack completely under water. He was eating lily pad roots. When I saw him, I paddled even more softly to see just how close I could get to this animal. He, of course, could not hear me and had to finally sense the vibration of the water. I must have been about 15 yards from him when he jerked his head up. I wish I'd had a camera to record that moment of lily pads and roots dripping from his rack. I'll never know how such a heavy animal can run so fast in water with a muddy bottom and a swampy shoreline.

I plan on seeing Emmert Holmes, one of the men who lived in the section house in Skibo at my time. He now lives in Two Harbors. It will be fun to see if he recalls what I do.

Emmert Holmes as a young man in the forests near Skibo.

CHAPTER 9

Nature's Wealth

Skibo and Fairbanks are in the heart of the fur country and being within the Superior National Forest, they were also in the heart of the large packs of timber wolves. During the summers of the 1920s and 1930s that I spent in Skibo, I became acquainted with professional trappers who still made a good living trapping for furs and bounties. I have learned that since those years, the county and state erased bounty-giving for wolves.

From my personal experience, when considering the handling of timber wolves in both Skibo and Fairbanks, one comes up with a most interesting difference between the 1920s and the 1990s. Seventy years ago, the wolf was the most profitable animal to trap or hunt, and maybe was the most talked-about wild animal when a group of men got together. Trappers found wolf trapping to be quite profitable since the county paid a $15 bounty, the state paid $15 more, and the hide was then worth an additional $18 to $25. I called one of my favorite game warden friends and asked him what the penalty is today if a trapper is caught with some wolf pelts. He told me that today, killing a wolf is a federal offense. He said the fine could go from $1,000 to considerably more, plus having to give up traps and guns. My friends and associates hated and despised wolves back then. Today, most of us like the animal and are happy to see one.

The cabin in which I was raised was in a dense pine forest that was full of wolves. I can clearly recall when I was about five years old sitting outside my cabin at night with a grown cousin who had a powerful flashlight. He would shine the light to the border of the forest so we could see wolves romping around. They never came close to us because, as I learned, wolves are wary of any bright lights. This really was fun. I so enjoy thinking about those wolves.

Much of my hunting was done with one of two second cousins. They were George James Huber and George Loren Huber. The latter and his father were with me once when we became lost and had to stay overnight on top of a high hill. This was about four miles from Fairbanks. It was cloudy and we had no way to determine which direction was home because I had no compass and they didn't know how to read theirs. We all were dressed too lightly for an overnight so we built a big fire for warmth and for protection from animals. After we got a big fire going, we "circled the wagons," as our pioneers would say, for the night.

We could not see well for we had no flashlights, but I became aware of animals I believed to be wolves. When it was my turn to sleep and George L. Huber's turn to stand guard, he woke me up. With great enthusiasm he told me to look at the sky, the stars were coming out. I was sort of the guide, as this was my home country we were hunting in, so I pointed at the North Star and told the other two to put out the fire for now we could head for home. I kept looking at that guiding light. We went straight to where I knew the railroad track was. After having a struggle fighting through three terrible swamps, we hit the railroad just as the sun was rising. We had one mile more to follow the railroad to home.

Another time, two of us were lost in the Superior National Forest five miles from Skibo, again while deer hunting. Just when it was time to sleep, we found what was probably a trapper's shack built somewhat like a root cellar. It had places to lie down, a stove and some wood. Our sleep was frequently disturbed by activity and sounds at the front door. We were afraid to open the door even though we slept close to it. It snowed during the night and in the morning we saw many wolf tracks near the door and at the corners of the shack. I could only assume that there was scent from wolves around because the trapper had skinned some. In the morning, in spite of considerable new snow, we found our way out of the forest and back to Skibo. There are not many men in our modern society who can say they slept within two feet of a pack of ferocious timber wolves.

Most of my hunting was done with George James Huber up the railroad toward Reno. I have also hunted with first cousins Frank Huber, George Huber and Jack Huber. I have, of course, done much hunting with friends who were not relatives. Many have left me for their "happy hunting ground." Those still living include Don Wilson, Karl Biebighauser, Don Davis, and Earl Clemment. Earl is the only one with whom I both hunted and trapped.

One of the pleasures I could have when deer hunting was not too productive. It was to walk the railroad between Skibo and Fairbanks and enjoy the packs of wolves howling at each other when the packs were over a mile apart. I suppose they threatened each other for the dominance of deer territory. I used to think that wolves howled mostly at night or at the moon. These experiences really gave a boy a good taste of wildlife among the large and aggressive animals.

Hunting pals Don Davis, John Lauerer and Earl Clemment (l-r) return from a successful pheasant hunting trip taken around 1945 near Skibo.

Joe (left) and John (right) Lauerer enjoyed fishing, trapping and hunting together in their youth.

It was quite common practice for young boys to hunt and trap wild animals. It was enjoyable and profitable. My brother Joe and I started trapping because the boys at school talked so much about it and had trapped animals before we had even tried.

It seemed Joe and I "trapped" much of the winter before we caught an animal. I was the first to catch anything, a white snowshoe rabbit. We skinned him and cleaned him for eating. Joe caught the first fur-bearing animal, a beautiful, white ermine. A somewhat elderly man who had been a hunter and trapper for years gave us one lesson on how to skin, stretch and dry the ermine. He gave us the lesson in his cabin.

In the years that followed, we caught all the furs important in the fur trade. There were muskrats and mink, and in later years, I caught beaver and martin.

Both of the large fur-trading companies had posts at Lake Vermilion, perhaps because of the plentiful supply of Minnesota's two most valuable fur-bearing animals, the fisher and the martin. Today, the trapping of martin is forbidden throughout nearly all of Minnesota, with only the extreme northern edge of St. Louis County and maybe just a bit of other counties in the Arrowhead allowing the taking of these animals.

When trapping, I check my traps at daylight so the animal does not suffer. Few people would believe that sometimes these animals seem to be asleep after they are caught. They are not jumping or trying to get loose and there is no mark where one would expect injury to the foot.

Once, I accidentally caught a fisher in a trap I had set for a mink. It was illegal then to trap fisher, so I reported that particular catch to the DNR. The law requires in such instances that the animal must be skinned, stretched and dried, and given to the DNR to be sold at auction. The trapper then gets half the money from the sale of the fur. The officer who picked up my pelt allowed me only half its value. He said my animal was shot, in spite of there not being any sign of a bullet hole. I received $8 from him for the pelting fee. A year or so later, fisher became legal to trap and I learned that these animals were bringing as much as $148. Some years ago, a man was caught by a game warden with over 20 fisher. In that year, fisher were either forbidden or the taking of only one was allowed. This man got off with a very light penalty, perhaps only a small fine. The treatment given to the man who killed over 20 fisher and to me who caught one by accident, gave a confession and did the work of skinning, stretching and drying, does not appear to be equal justice.

By far the most interesting fur-bearing animal is the ermine. It is ferocious and a killer. Only by having chickens does one know how the ermine will kill most of a large brood thought to be safely perched in a securely closed barn. Ermine do not kill for meat, but for blood and fun. I have seen more than 10 grown hens killed by an ermine who made a hole in the neck and sucked the blood out of the bird without doing the least injury to any of the meat on the hen's body. The pious judges of Europe could not have picked a meaner animal to symbolize their position and rank. The ermine's fur serves not only as an emblem of honor and purity for judges, but also for kings, queens and other members of the nobility. Ermine have one of the shortest life spans of any four-footed mammal — I believe less than two years. This short life span causes the

John Lauerer with 15 ermine pelts he took on his trap line.

ermine population to fluctuate. I haven't seen an ermine track in years, yet some years they are numerous.

We sent most of our furs to St. Louis. It is easy to think that the lucrative fur trade with the Indians was sometimes unfair. Not so the trading today. Nearly all fur-buying companies will hold a trapper's furs separate until they are sure you have accepted the price.

I could not discuss hunting and trapping without emphasizing the need for safety and training, and the importance of being sure of the correct target before pulling the trigger. A wonderful hunter-trapper got me started in gun safety when I first started hunting; I give Charlie Heckbarth credit for 700 youths whose lives I touched and whose behavior was modified because of attending the hunter safety classes I taught.

The way Charlie talked to me about gun handling, loading, unloading, and always making sure to point the gun in a safe direction made such an impression on me that I decided to get trained as a qualified fire arms safety instructor.

In these classes, I also did work on water safety, compass work, and even driving safety. It is some thrill to have a middle-aged man come to me and tell me that he took gun safety from me and how much that has meant to him.

Charlie was a good teacher about pointing, loading and carrying guns, yet he actually pointed his powerful deer rifle right at another hunter and shot him in the crotch. This happened several miles from Fairbanks where there was no paramedic, no pain killer, no litter carrier and no blood or plasma available. The victim survived, but was crippled for life. The shooter suffered, too, and was mentally never the same man again.

As in many accidents, the victim may have been a little at fault since in the 1920s, the bright orange clothing used in

Charlie Heckbarth lived a half-block from the Fairbanks school and was an avid hunter.

hunting today was not required. The victim was cleaning out a dear on a rock. Most likely there was not sufficient bright red on his clothing or around the rock for Charlie to distinguish the man who was cleaning the deer.

John Lauerer displays a prize catch from the waters near Fairbanks and Skibo.

CHAPTER 10

A Determined Effort

One picture in my possession is of the 1928 football team at Eveleth Junior College. It shows me in the front row. The Eveleth team belonged to the "Little Ten League" made up of junior colleges and teacher's colleges in the state. This team had much the same members as the 1929 team. The latter team has both good and bad history.

The 1929 team was the best in years. It beat, by big scores, all the teams it played. Late in the season, we had one team,

The 1929 Eveleth Junior College football squad. Bottom row (left to right): Paul Christian, right end; John Maki, left end; Hjalmer Jacobson, right tackle; Robert Nelson, right guard; Robert Segal, captain and left halfback; Joe Rebrovich, center; Carl Skoog, left guard; Nelo Jacobson, left tackle; Gordon Broman, left end. Middle Row: C.R. Thompson, assistant coach; Charley Mattson, right halfback; Walter DePaul, right halfback; Rudolph Usnik, fullback; Leslie Knuti, quarterback; John Grahek, quarterback; John Lauerer, left tackle; J.O. Christian, coach. Top row: Charles Manella, left halfback; Cyril Tousignant, halfback and full back; William Mattson, right tackle; Clarence Schoultz, right guard; Joe Lauerer, center; Arne Leskinen, right end; Edwin Rauma, left guard; Kenneth Pihlstrom, fullback; Edward Halonen, student manager.

the Virginia Junior College, left to play. They had lost almost every game by rather big scores. In the minds of most of our players, because Virginia was thought to be a pushover, we already believed ourselves to be the state champs. In fact, some were already planning a victory banquet. Furthermore, there were copies of gold footballs circulating around the college halls so we could pick the kind of footballs we thought were good enough for players like us to wear.

Our dear coach, who worked so hard for weeks to make us champs, smelled a rat and was worried. He gave us the best chalk talk the night before the game, trying his very best to convince us that we had a very tough game to play the next day. His aim was to take that cocky over-confidence out of our minds. He tried so hard, talking about the two good running backs we would be facing the next day, saying that to stop them would require our best effort.

Apparently, as happens so often, the coach's words went in one ear and out the other. Some boys must have had a pregame victory party late at night before game day. As I was walking out on the field of play, I noticed on the footpath that a number of boys must have had sick stomachs for they left considerable food, mostly canned corn, on the ground.

Eveleth could do nothing against Virginia. They beat us 14 to zero. I would pay considerable money for a video tape of the locker room after that game. There was very little talk, but plenty of crying and dripping tears.

I particularly noticed the biggest, most rugged player that one would say could never cry, let out his emotions the greatest. I saw this kid play a high school game before he came to college. He played without a helmet. He had the biggest crop of heavy, wire-like hair. Maybe no helmet in high school would fit his hair and head.

One late afternoon, we were having a football scrimmage at Eveleth Junior College on top of a hill near the water tank. Suddenly, a loud crack was heard by some people. Actually, the sound came from a break in my brother Joe's leg. The coach looked at Joe's leg and ordered the poor fellow to run around the race track a couple of times. He, of course, could not obey such a ridiculous command. X-rays taken the next day revealed the break, and Joe had to wear a full cast and walk with crutches for a number of weeks. Perhaps this "evil" of football was the reason my parents would not allow us to play the game in high school.

Our coach worked with the Eveleth Junior College football team for years. He was a likable man and a good coach, but did have a temper. One day, at practice, he told a player to get down on his knee in a football stance. When the player obeyed, the coach gave the poor team member the most awful kick on his posterior anatomy. One day during scrimmage, I happened to say just a few words to another player. The coach gave me a lecture to the effect that if I would pay attention, maybe, in many years to come, I might become a football player.

Since my parents had not allowed me to play football in high school, I had rough going at first in college. I did like the sport and worked hard at it right from the start, but competition from those who had years of experience in high school required real effort on my part. After a week or two, one afternoon during scrimmage, things happened in my favor.

After my success at stopping a gain around my end by the first team, the coach lost his temper, I guess. The coach, without a helmet and with little, if any, padding, called a play where he got the ball. The play called was straight at my territory. Well, I tackled the bare-headed coach before he crossed the line. I recall hitting him hard and throwing the slight, small man with his face and bare head against the hard clay turf. In the 1920s, fields did not have the cushion of grass. The coach was a determined little fellow. He tried again at least two more times. On none of his attempts did he gain yardage in my territory of the defense.

I soon was given much play time. I recall starting one game in which I was played the full 60 minutes, both offense and defense, because at the time there was very little platoon system played. Before much longer, I had earned a letter, which really thrilled me to no end. Most athletes would call this some accomplishment. I still have the sweater and letter I earned.

At a college reunion decades later, I saw that coach again.

Did the sight of him ever start memories rolling out of my mind! When it came time to be seated for the banquet, my wife and I ended up at the same table as that dear coach. In fact, I sat across the table from him. Alas, I was in for the greatest disappointment of the evening, and if I had not been surrounded by so many nice people, I would have cried. The coach could not remember me nor any of his many years in lovely Eveleth. He had Alzheimer's and it was impossible to carry on a conversation with him.

CHAPTER 11

My Best Dream Come True

In order to get through college at Hamline University in St. Paul, I took a job for one dollar a day running two dishwashers in downtown St. Paul at a rather luxurious nighttime dining place that was actually underground and called the Dugout. The owner and boss of the Dugout was president of the Minnesota Restaurant Association at the time. My hours were 5:00 p.m. to 1:00 a.m. At times, I would walk home to the college fraternity, Kappa Gamma Chi, when I could not afford the streetcar fare, which I remember being about a dime.

When New Year's Eve approached, I was commanded, not asked, to work until closing, about 4:00 a.m. I washed few dishes after 1:00 a.m. while others were having good times. Even though I was dressed in my rough work clothes, I was not always in the back room with the dishes, but sometimes in the luxurious dining room with the finely-dressed people. Mostly, I was in the rest rooms mopping up the food and liquor with which some customers had overfilled their stomachs.

Of course I was glad to get the extra hours. I expected to get double time in my weekly pay envelope. I didn't get it; nor time and a half. Not even regular pay for the three additional hours was included in my paycheck.

What could I do or say? I was afraid if I complained I would be fired and maybe have to drop out of college. If there had been a union steward I would have had someone to speak up for me. If people had rights then as they have rights today, the handling I received might have been considered a violation of my rights.

In later years, some people thought of me as anti-union. They were basing this only on my executive-level position. To such an accusation, my answer was quick. If there had been good unions when I was growing up, my life and my work life would have been better.

It is a good thing that the experiences of my growing up on the Range gave me the strength, mental acuity and forbearance to compete in the workplace and survive the Twin Cities' corporate rat race. My folks repeatedly told me when I finished college and started on a full-time regular job to not move around from job to job. So when I started making progress and getting increases, I felt good.

After about 20 years, when one of my superiors was on vacation, I used my judgment instead of being a "yes" man. As a result, I was demoted from my good job and my salary was cut in half. Driving home that night I could have cried, but after telling my wife and getting her positive response, I felt better. I began to think what my reaction to my problem should be and thought of something positive.

I majored in history in college and was qualified to teach at the high school level, so I applied in person for a job to teach the Constitution and Government to immigrants so they could qualify for U.S. citizenship. I was hired immediately to work part-time two nights a week with a good hourly rate. The job was fun, and probably because I also was foreign, I received a good response from my students. I had as many as 34 students in one class and over the years, taught students from 20 different countries.

My big job with the corporation changed. After I resold myself and my abilities to a new superior, I was given additional responsibility and much more pay than I had before I was demoted. In fact, I had titles over two departments, accuracy control and quality control. The work the men and women under my supervision did sometimes had an impact at the other eight facilities, as well as our local one for the Midwest region. At times, some of the "discoveries" or suggestions coming from my department even had an impact on the 400 smaller units in the nation from coast to coast, not to mention the foreign countries from which we often imported merchandise.

I was now making more than enough to feed the children. I told my wife that I enjoyed my night teaching so much that I would continue even though the income from it was no longer needed to finance the needs of the children. I would keep the teaching income in a separate account and let it accumulate interest, which was considerable in those days. I would use this as my "gambling money," but not in casinos or with cards or slot machines. I would play with the safest investment there is: I would buy and sell tax-delinquent lakeshore timberland. The amount of lakeshore timberland available at state auction sales in the 1960s was unbelievable. St. Louis County had the most, and on lakes that were some of my favorite playgrounds.

I bought four large tracts of tax-delinquent lands that were offered on the land auction in the Duluth courthouse. As an example, I bought 50 acres at one of my favorite lakes from the state for $160 and sold it to the Federal Government for $14,000. Actually, I did not have to sell it. The Federal land buyer came to my wife and me at the auction sale. I even bought the choicest piece of Lake Superior shoreline with large evergreen trees, about three acres, for $7,000. This was not tax delinquent but on an estate sale. I sold the Lake Superior property for $31,000. I did not leave out my dear Iron Range — I bought 50 acres with huge pine trees on Pine Island in Lake Vermilion for $600. I have had a cabin built on it for about $35,000. Today the place is worth $75,000.

My luck with land soon traveled around the gossip circle in the corporation. I suppose some wondered how a department head who got demoted one year could develop such financial brain power two years later.

One night at a "profit party" the top big shot of the business sought me out and had me sit with him at a table. He admired all the talk he heard about "little me" and asked that I tell him what I did so he could do likewise.

I gritted my teeth, looked him in both eyes and pointed my finger squarely at his eyes. I said, "Do you remember a few years ago when you approved a disastrous demotion for me and a cutting of my salary in half? Well Mr. Trepp, that was the best damned thing that you ever did for me." Then I told him how I capitalized on the condemning action of me that he approved.

My work with immigrants continued for decades. It was so

much fun. I taught the U.S. Constitution to about 1,000 immigrants who became U.S. citizens. I loved these students, and sensed that they loved me.

The most unusual aspect of most of these immigrant people was their history, living problems and abuse. These people told me so much, sometimes with tears. They related to me well because I, too, was a foreigner whose family came here, although for a different reason.

What thrilled me the most was the opportunity to make use of some of the psychology I had learned in college. Occasionally, there would be a student, most often a female, who would be afraid of the other students and their instructor. This was more common with some ethnic groups than others. Some women displayed an extreme inferiority complex. In such a case, I would tell my boss that I had almost a "dead" student whom I could not bring to life and I would have to just give that student an attendance certificate. If I had time, I would wait for a chance to work with a student and possibly to work wonders.

If ever there was a time when a student like this might answer a question that nobody else knew or when others were slow to react, I would praise this person more than usual and say, "How in the world was so-and-so so smart to do what others could not?" If such a case happened again down the road, I would repeat my praising. Often, this kind of handling would bring fantastic results and help the person crawl out of his or her shell.

I remember at least one such case where the problem student actually got the highest mark in the class on her finals and went on to pass the test given her by the Government. Furthermore, at a party to celebrate newly-acquired citizenship, one student, who was originally very shy, talked to many people, including the lieutenant governor, and was very graceful.

One morning after the **Minneapolis Tribune** had carried a two-page article along with photos showing my work with the foreign born, I received a phone call from the president of the oldest college in our state. He told me how he admired the work I was doing and asked my permission to place the story in the Hamline University Archives. I never dreamed the work

I had done to save my family from financial disaster would bring the rewarding and surprising results it did.

If there was any fault in my teaching, I perhaps praised our wonderful democracy too much. There are so many examples of government failure and so many times when our government only takes steps to correct problems after our news media points them out. Perhaps I should have prepared my students for some of the evils of our system. Nevertheless, my teaching helped many people on their way to reaching their hopes and dreams, and in the process, it helped to make my best possible dreams come true.

CHAPTER 12

Safety First

My mother exerted a powerful influence upon my life. Two of the most important lessons she taught me were not to do anything to excess and to always be safety-minded. In later years, these were to be very important to me.

Shortly after my wife and I were married, we went on a honeymoon trip to Lake Louise and Banff in the Canadian Rockies. On the way home, as we were driving through Idaho with another couple, we stopped for supper before driving on to the town in which we were to spend the night.

As we planned our menu for this special meal, we all considered having some highballs, but as I sat there, my mother's image kept coming to mind. If she were here in person, she would tell about the danger of consuming alcohol when I planned to continue driving afterward. I told my wife and friends I would take no drinks.

Later, while en route to our destination for the night, my abstinence paid off. A car swerved into our lane as it approached us. I calmly pulled my 1936 Pontiac onto the shoulder before the opposing driver glanced off our vehicle. We suffered little damage and no injuries but in the other car, three people were killed. If I had not refused the drink, we likely would have been killed as well.

As I grew older, I became a real "safety nut." I taught more than 700 young men gun safety because I so wanted them to be able to experience the thrill of the outdoors and to do so in a safe manner. I have followed up on many of them and nothing thrills me more than to hear them tell me how valuable their gun safety training has been.

As a young boy, the sawmill at Fairbanks and its remarkable safety record made quite a significant impression on me. Because of this, in later life, I followed with considerable interest the progress of logging and lumbering in our western states. As a result of my study and interest in this subject, I discovered that the Virginia Rainy Lake Mill has had one of the best safety records over the years. I was not too favorably impressed with the Pacific Mill in Scotia, Calif., however, and for good reason.

On August 6, 1991, my wife and I were returning from California after visiting our daughter and her family. I learned that we were driving toward Scotia, where the Pacific Lumber Company has the largest redwood sawmill in the country. I made arrangements to get a tour through that mill. What a thrill I looked forward to. Now, I could check all the modern workers and compare with those who were so full of fun communicating in pantomime with me when I was a kid. Most of all, I wanted to see the tail sawyer and compare his working with that of my dad's and to see the sawyer working, since that is the most important job in the mill.

What a disappointment the tour turned out to be! The entire mill was automated. It was run and controlled by computers. I only saw one man at work. He appeared to be a floor sweeper. He criticized me for stepping over the line where tourists were supposed to walk.

I asked a man where all the workers were. He replied that they were off by themselves in a room punching keys where they could not be seen. They were all punching keys! At Scotia, all these workers spend the entire work day doing nothing but punching keys that activate the machines and saws. Apparently, even the huge carriage with sometimes huge logs is run forward and backward, controlled by keys.

The stations where I expected smiles, waving hands and pantomime were so empty and lonely. I did not see any of the key punchers, but I doubt whether they had much to smile about, as the men did at Fairbanks.

My research after the tour revealed that a loud whistle is blown every 20 minutes and the work is stopped so the workers can relax a bit before continuing the stressful key punching. Apparently this repetitive, unsatisfying work is terribly hard on even young, healthy workers.

From what I saw and was told, the operators were not able to see much of the logs and boards as they worked. I saw no smiling faces and no happy men having fun as they worked, like I did in the Fairbanks mill.

Over the years, I have remained interested in the Pacific Lumber Company mill at Scotia. In 1992, the Division of Occupational Safety and Health in San Francisco reported that three men were killed in the Pacific mill at Scotia. The accident was reported by the ***Minneapolis Tribune*** on Sept. 19, 1992.

Mill accident kills 3 in California
Associated Press

Scotia, Calif. A log processing machine in a wood chip mill apparently started up while three workers were inside it, killing them, authorities said Wednesday.

The victims were found inside a large machine that strips bark from logs, Pacific Lumber spokeswoman Mary Bullwinkle said. The "debarker" is a large rotating drum.

The workers apparently were trying to unclog the machine by turning it off and going in with chain saws to cut away a jam, said Richard Stephens, a spokesman for the California Division of Occupational Safety and Health in San Francisco.

I recently secured a copy of OSHA's 14-page investigation summary from that accident and feel compelled to type a letter about safety and accidents in the American workplace.

I have also studied meat packing plants and learned additional information from a cousin of mine. He was a German immigrant who had to make a living at a very stressful, boring job He was also the victim of speed and modern technology. If I remember correctly, he was expected to prepare several hundred hogs an hour for hanging on the overhead conveyor. His job was to slit the hind legs to expose the tendons so the hogs could hang on the hooks of the conveyor. He drank more alcohol than I did, no doubt because of his job-related stress, and he died an untimely, early death.

It seems that often the best thing that can be said for many American companies is their speed for profit. I suppose this is progress, but progress toward what? Only to see more profit for the owner? I suppose this is desirable in one sense, but such repetitive monotony might be the cause for some of society's problems: Too hurried life, fast driving under congested traffic, the excessive use of alcohol and other drugs — in short, not enough true relaxing and a sense of boredom.

I am convinced that some of the problems we are experiencing as a nation are the result of stress. We are first in the world in violent deaths. We are plagued with problems in our society due to alcohol and drug abuse. Rape and murder increase more and more rapidly every day. These things do not happen because God has made meaner men here than elsewhere.

We Americans spend much money and time and effort training young men and women to become professional killers in the military. Then, when they complete their work for Uncle Sam and their killing days have ended, they are expected to return to a non-killing world with no deprogramming. In the military, they arc praised for killing. Now, if they kill in a fit of temper that arouses some of their wartime response, they are imprisoned. I believe we owe it to these young people to retrain them as peaceful citizens before sending them back home to their families and jobs.

If we could slow down our industrial complex so the men and women who work in our factories and offices could get just a morsel of fun out of their striving for money for themselves and their companies, maybe less harm would result and our country could become a safer place to live.

If somehow the terrible stress and monotony of our workers could be reduced 20 percent, perhaps workers could occasionally smile like my dad and his working companions did eight decades ago in that Fairbanks sawmill.

I Remember Fairbanks and Skibo

Epilogue

In many ways, I have lived the history of the United States and the American dream. My family came to America as immigrants from Europe, poor in material wealth perhaps, but full of the spirit, hopes and dreams so common among the hardy souls that struck out for the "new world."

And a new world it was! My family lived the frontier experience of America in the white pine forests, even down to the log cabin where we settled; and it was labor on the land, taming the wilderness and harvesting the vast natural resources of the continent for the use of an industrializing economy that put food on our table. Of course, this work and these resources also provided the means for me to earn a college education.

Just as the United States was able to build upon the frontier experience to industrialize and become a world leader in business, so was I able to build upon the experiences of my youth and become a successful businessman as Catalog Operations Quality and Accuracy Control Manager for Montgomery Ward at their headquarters in St. Paul, Minn. Furthermore, I was able to draw upon my roots in the North Woods during times of economic adversity to not only maintain my family's economic independence, but with the encouragement of my wife, to secure my family's financial future.

It has been so rewarding to assist other immigrants in getting their citizenship and setting them on their own course in America. Just as happened for my family so many years ago, many new immigrants still come each year to the United States to seek their fortune and a new future. I am proud to think I may have made it easier for some of them to succeed in their new lives as American citizens.

It has been even more rewarding for me to work as a volunteer safety instructor, teaching the youth of our state the importance of gun and hunting safety. I say more rewarding because in my opinion, nothing could be more worthwhile than time spent with our youth in recreation.

Looking back, as I frequently do, on the experiences of more than 80 years, I am struck by the amazing changes that have occurred in my lifetime. Most of these have been changes for the better and certainly we would not want to give up the conveniences of modern life. Other changes, of course, leave me pondering where we are headed, or rather, where young people today will find themselves should they achieve my age.

My father would never have accepted hand-outs. He started in logging work by loading ties in rail cars the first week he lived in this country. Very soon, he started working in the sawmill, which he enjoyed ever so much until the mill closed down a decade later. Still he did not give up, as do many who find themselves unexpectedly without work today. He never gave up, but worked to support his family in a dignified way.

It is of great concern to me that the family structure that was so important to my upbringing continues to disintegrate in American society. True, my father was a stern man with many responsibilities outside the home and who, perhaps, participated less than he should have in the nurturing aspects of child rearing, but, my mother more than compensated for his lack. In fact, my mother had more control over me than my dear daddy, whose behavior, no doubt, was like most of the men who had the military training for killing others with the German Kaiser's military efficiency.

My mother was so gentle, so calm, so mild, so loving, and I give her credit for nurturing the character traits that caused me to become a defensive driver and saved the lives of the four people in my car the night of that horrible accident near the Bitterroot Mountains. My daddy, on the other hand, was an excellent provider and instilled in us a great sense of discipline which has proved invaluable to me throughout my life. Together, they provided the balance so necessary in raising a boy who not only saved himself from the world's temptations and dangers, but also made himself a law-abiding man.

Today, many children live in single-parent homes, and are robbed of the benefit of having a second parent to balance

Theresa and Joseph on their wedding day

whatever weaknesses the other parent may have. Worse, they may be robbed of nurturing because the single parent has to work so hard to be the economic provider, thus leaving many children with no "nurture provider" whatsoever.

It is of much deeper concern to me that people seem to care much less about each other than we did in my youth. We had less crime then. Today, crime is perhaps the number one concern of our society. People seemed more honest then and more wholesome. Of course, we didn't have electronic media beaming all the evils of our world into our homes either. It's probably at least partly true that our world was not much better than the world today, but simply that we were more innocent then

81

and because of our innocence, freer to indulge in small pleasures. This is perhaps the greatest change I could note, and the change I most regret for young people today.

In any case, Fairbanks and Skibo, like the days of my youth, are no more. These memories I have recorded may be the only thing that is written about them. It is my hope and prayer that in recording my memories of that place and time, I will have provided at least some small record for future generations of what it was like to live in such a special place.